Wetlands

A HARPERCOLLINS NATURE STUDY BOOK

Wetlands

by Ronald Rood

illustrated by Marlene Hill Donnelly

HarperCollins*Publishers*

Also in the HarperCollins Nature Study Series:
Backyard Birds / Tide Pools

And the parched ground shall become a pool,
and the thirsty land springs of water: in the
habitation of dragons, where each lay, shall be
grass with reeds and rushes.
—Isaiah 35:7

Wetlands
Text copyright © 1994 by Ronald Rood
Illustrations copyright © 1994 by Marlene Hill Donnelly
For information address HarperCollins Children's Books, a division of
HarperCollins Publishers, 10 East 53rd Street, New York, NY 10022.
Library of Congress Cataloging-in-Publication Data
Rood, Ronald N.
    Wetlands / by Ronald Rood ; illustrated by Marlene Hill Donnelly.
        p.   cm. — (HarperCollins nature study book)
    Summary: Introduces the many kinds of plants and animals found in fresh-
water wetlands, including flycatchers, whirligig beetles, and tiny water fleas
and worms.
    ISBN 0-06-023010-X. — ISBN 0-06-023011-8 (lib. bdg.)
    1. Wetlands—Juvenile literature.   2. Wetland fauna—Juvenile literature.
3. Wetland plants—Juvenile literature.   [1. Wetlands.   2. Wetland animals.
3. Wetland plants.]   I. Donnelly, Marlene Hill, ill.   II. Title.   III. Series.
QH87.3.R65   1994   92-47140
574.5'26325—dc20   CIP
                                                                                     AC
1   2   3   4   5   6   7   8   9   10
❖
First Edition

Contents

Watery World

If you look down from an airplane or tall building, nothing seems to be going on below. People and animals are just tiny specks. Cars hardly move. Yet everything is really still there.

Swamps and streams and soggy places may seem like that, too. They appear to be only water and weeds. Is there anything of interest in such a squelchy wasteland?

Yes indeed. Go to the water's edge. Squat down and look. You may find plants

that move. There may be creatures that walk on water, breathe by means of snorkels, or send their jaws out for lunch.

Discover these living things, and many more, with the help of this book. Explore a swampy area, a slow-moving stream, a soggy abandoned lot. Such places, with grass and weeds and shallow water, are called freshwater wetlands. Other books tell about salty wetlands near the seashore.

Get a magnifying glass. Try making the microscope described in these pages. Then take this book as your guide through the wonderful, watery world of the wetlands.

The Water's Edge

You can often tell when you're getting near fresh water. It is cooler there. The air may smell cleaner. There may be many plants and animals that can be found nowhere else.

Much of this freshness is due to the trees and other plants that live there. They soak up moisture and pass it out through their leaves. Along with green algae, or pond scum, they give off oxygen needed by air-breathing animals.

Many plants stand right in the

mud, just as you may do as you explore their watery homes. Cattail plants often grow in shallow water. They may be taller than a person, with long, fuzzy brown tops, called spikes, looking like burned hot dogs on sticks. Native Americans used the fluffy seeds in these spikes as padding for their cradles. They also showed the settlers how to weave mats from the leaves and make flour from the roots.

Wetlands serve as nurseries for many birds. The brown swamp grass hides their nests. There are insects and berries to eat. Prairie ponds, called potholes, can be homes for thousands of ducks and geese. Herons and other long-legged wading birds

look for fish and frogs in the shallows. Their small cousins the sandpipers poke their beaks into the mud for worms and insects.

Baby raccoons may walk behind their ring-tailed mother as if playing follow the leader. With their little black masks, they look like a line of clowns. If they find a frog or tasty worm, they rub it around in the wa-

ter as if it needed washing. A raccoon will even wash a fish, though the fish has been in water all its life.

Frogs sit at the water's edge, waiting for insects. In the spring you can hear some of them croaking as others lay their jellylike egg masses in the water. Baby frogs, called tadpoles or pollywogs, seem to be only a chubby body, a tail, and a little mouth that

looks puckered up in a kiss. As they
grow, tadpoles develop legs and lose
their tails. At last they become like
their parents: wide-mouthed, goggle-
eyed, jumping frogs.

Turtles bask in sunny places on
the shore, or on logs and other ob-
jects that poke out above the water.
They began life as soft-shelled eggs
in the sand near the water. Turtles

have keen eyesight, so approach them carefully. They may be slow on land, but they're quick to drop into the water. Then all you will see is a splash.

All these living things and many others may be neighbors in a wetland. They are brought together by the two worlds of land and water—getting some of each, there at the water's edge.

The Living Skies

Swamps and other squishy wet-lands are busy night and day. Even the air above them seems filled with life. Insects that spend their early days below the surface may leave their watery homes. They develop wings and fly away in search of mates. Soon they will lay their eggs.

One familiar wetland dweller is the mosquito. It may give us an itchy bite, but it is important as food for many of its neighbors. Wriggling through the water like an active little caterpillar, the young mosquito is hunted by fish and other water dwellers. In the air, adult mosquitos may be caught by swallows and other birds or by night-flying bats.

The graceful swallow darts and zooms, catching many flying insects. When it has a mouthful, the swallow takes the insects back to its babies. Look for the blue-backed tree swallow's home in a hollow tree near the

water. Grayish birds known as fly-catchers sit on a branch, watching for mosquitoes or other insects. You can hear a flycatcher's beak snap as it captures its flying food in midair.

Dragonflies also catch hundreds of mosquitoes. Often brightly col-ored, dragonflies zoom like little four-winged airplanes above the wa-ter. As it goes, the dragonfly holds its

bristly legs together to form a basket
for catching other insects.

Damselflies also hold their legs
like baskets to catch insects. Like
their larger cousins the dragonflies,
damselflies may be red or green or
other colors. At rest, they hold their
wings upright, not out to the side like
dragonflies. Both insects eat as they
fly, as you may eat an apple while
walking.

One of the strangest water dramas

is lived by the mayfly. After many months as a silvery-looking creature that can swim like a fish, the mayfly nymph, as it is called, leaves the water. Shedding its skin, it develops wings and flies away to find a mate. Within a few hours (or at most a few days) the female lays her eggs and dies. Since mayflies live just a short time after leaving the water, they do not need to eat. Many adult mayflies do not even have a stomach!

Top of the Water

Try this experiment: Gently lay a needle or straight pin on the surface of a pan of water. Placed perfectly flat, it will float. The surface of the water actually bends a little and holds up a light weight.

This strength is known as "surface tension." It allows some creatures to walk on water and others to cling to the surface from below. When air gets beneath water, surface tension can form a bubble.

One common top walker is the water strider. Half an inch long, it looks like a slender gray twig with legs.

Four of its six legs are much longer than the front two and make dimples on the surface as it skates on the water. These dimples catch the sunlight and make bright spots on the bottom.

The stretchy water surface is a raceway for the speedy whirligig beetle. Looking like an active watermelon seed, this shiny black insect zips around in circles on the surface. Its eyes are in two parts: One sees upward while the other looks down toward the bottom. Like the water strider, this beetle catches unlucky

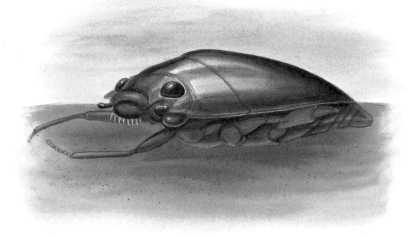

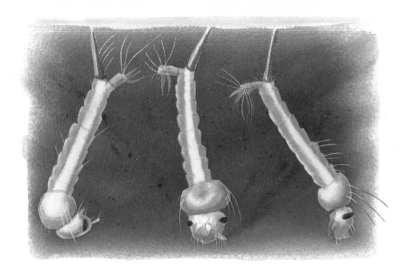

insects that have fallen onto the water from above.

Mosquito eggs float on the surface in little clusters. When they hatch, the swimming larvae, or wigglers, breathe through special snorkel tubes that bring air down from the surface above.

The water can support much larger creatures as well. Tails up and heads down, ducks and geese reach to the bottom for their food. Air trapped in their feathers helps them

to float. The longer necks and larger bodies of geese allow them to reach deeper than ducks. Both ducks and geese feed on snails and worms and water plants in the mud.

One favorite food of these web-footed birds is a tiny floating plant called duckweed. Its little round leaves may be only the size of this letter *o*. Sometimes thousands of these plants may cover a pool like a solid green blanket.

You may find other plants and animals on the surface of the water. Look just below the surface for an insect with two long legs like the oars of a tiny rowboat. This back swimmer, as it is called, takes a bubble of air with it to breathe as it dives. Then, true to its name, it swims along upside down.

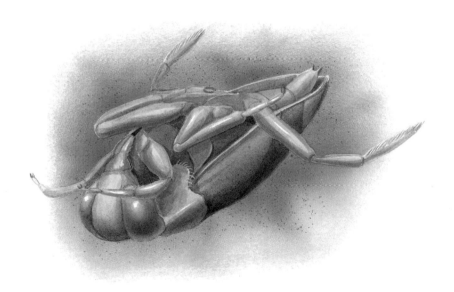

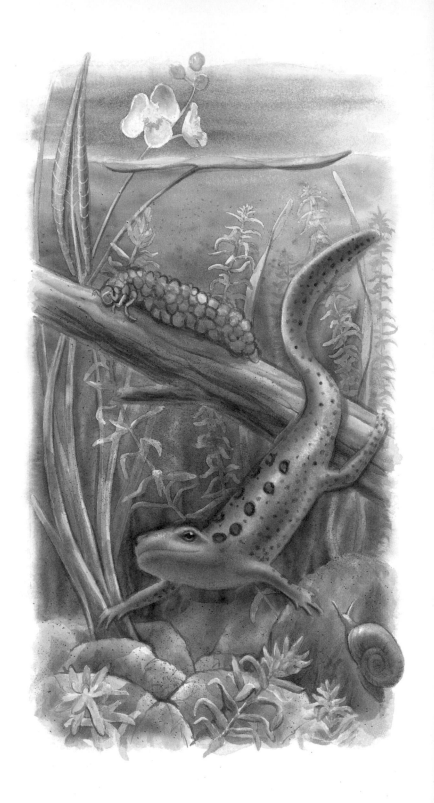

In the Depths

There is a busy world below the surface of a wetland pool. Many fish from large ponds and streams pay a visit to lay their eggs in the shallows. Their babies hide and feed in the pools until they are big enough to venture out into deeper water.

Many salamanders lay their eggs in these wetlands as well. Some live in water all their lives, while others hide under old logs and stones on land. Some salamanders may be spotted, or black, or brown. Many look like tiny alligators or lizards. Salamanders are harmless and

couldn't hurt you if they tried. You
may see the little red eft salamander
on a moist country path and find it
next year in a wetland pool. When it
becomes an adult, it changes from
red to greenish-brown with a yellow
stomach.

Look for the little caddisworm on
sunken sticks and rocks. It glues tiny
twigs or sand grains together to

build a sort of tube or cabin half an inch long. It lives inside this cabin, reaching out of it and dragging it along wherever it goes.

When full grown, the caddisworm turns into a flying creature looking like a little brown moth. Most moths hold their wings out to the side when at rest, however, while caddisflies fold their wings over their backs like little tents.

Down at the bottom you may see a mud-colored blob, half the size of your little finger, creeping toward a baby fish. It is a young dragonfly nymph, about to send its jaws out for dinner. These jaws are on an extra flap below its mouth. It thrusts the flap forward, but the jaws miss the fish. Next time it may be more fortunate, for this is the way the slow-

moving nymph can catch active swimming creatures.

Snails glide along the bottom, scraping tiny plants, called algae, from rocks and old logs. Put a snail in a glass of water and you'll see its tongue going in and out, in and out — scraping at the glass.

Long green threads of algae, called pond scum, grow in the depths

too. So does eel grass, with long, rib-bonlike leaves. Arrowhead leaves poke up from the bottom into the air above.

Muskrats can be found in almost any swampy area. These furry cousins of the mouse are as big as cats, with long, slender tails. They like to dive to the bottom and bring

up food—a freshwater mussel, perhaps. They also eat cattails and other plants, and live in houses made from mounds of grass and cattail leaves.

These living things—and many more—can be found where there is a little water. They are almost unknown and unseen, unless you look for them in the wonderful wetlands.

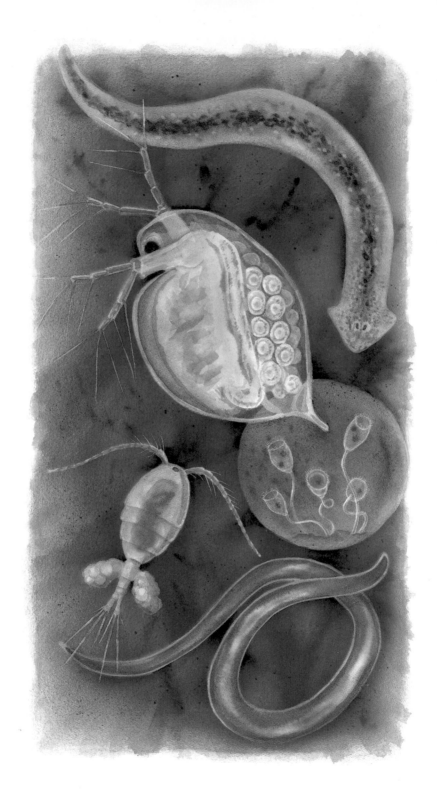

A Closer Look

Remember starting this book by getting down and meeting the soggy places at their own level? You can get even closer with a magnifying glass. A pint of muddy water from a swamp bottom can show you a surprising world.

There is the water flea, for instance. Its shell may be so transparent that you can see its beating heart. The cyclops, with one central eye, resembles a tiny lobster with no claws as it swims jerkily along. A little roundworm whips back and forth like an active letter *s*. A flatworm

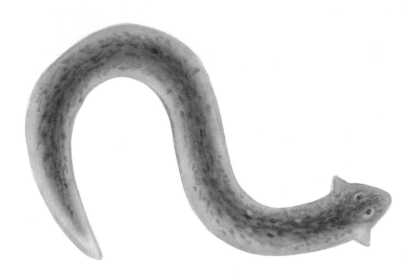

glides along like a snail with no shell.

For more surprises, make your own microscope. It is simple to use, but a little help from an adult may be needed to get it made just right. Using scissors, cut a ½-inch-wide, 3-inch-long strip from a sturdy plastic tub, such as those used for margarine or cottage cheese. Round off the corners. Have an adult help you drill a 3/32-inch hole about half an inch from one end. Make sure the hole has no ragged edges.

With a toothpick held straight up, place a drop of water *exactly* in the hole. The water's surface tension will form the drop into a perfect little ball in the hole. This makes a clear, high-powered lens. And there's your microscope!

Practice using your "scope" on a

torn bit of wet newspaper stuck to a window. Microscopes work only at close range, so get half an inch away from the newspaper. With the scope to your eye, look at the paper's torn edge. You will see the fibers magnified nearly a hundred times.

For the microscope's stage, attach an extension cord to a small light fixture, such as an electric Christmas candle or a night light, and put it in a strong cardboard box with a hole for the light to come through.

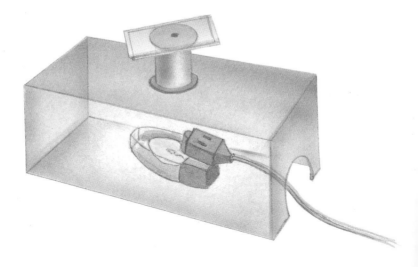

Glue a spool from a large spool of sewing thread to the box so the light will shine up through the hole. Two flat rectangular pieces of glass hold the specimen in place.

Drop a bit of muddy water on one glass slide and cover it with the other. Turn on the light. Slowly bend down

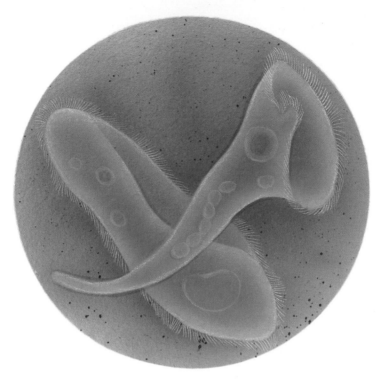

with your scope until the water drop comes into focus. And there's a new world!

There'll be ciliates, swimming by means of tiny hairs, or cilia. Rotifers creep along like caterpillars or stretch like rubber. Tiny algae, or diatoms, have beautiful shapes and colors like jewels. Some of them move along like little boats.

These and many other forms of life help feed water insects and little fish. The fish and insects are eaten by larger fish and frogs, who are eaten by birds and mammals. It all starts in the ripples and shallows of the wonderful wetlands—right there at your muddy feet.

Looking Down on a Wetland
Our artist made this sketch of a wetland and its inhabitants near her home.

tadpoles taking cover
under lily pads

great white heron

dragonfly

ducks feeding
in shallow water

You can sketch a wetland that you find nearby too!

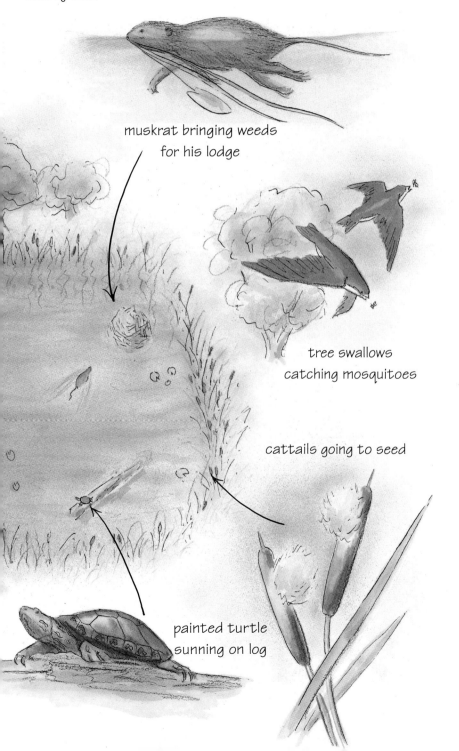

muskrat bringing weeds for his lodge

tree swallows catching mosquitoes

cattails going to seed

painted turtle sunning on log

Would You Like to Know More?

No single book could ever tell the whole story of the wetlands. Each swamp or pool or marsh is different from any other. Beavers may make a new pond in a week by building a dam across a stream in a meadow. A flood can wash away a dam overnight while the rushing water makes a new pond somewhere else. Here are a few books with more stories of the world of the wetlands.

Catlin, Stephen. *Wonders of Swamps and Marshes*. Mahwah, NJ: Troll Associates, 1990.

Chulland, Helen. *Disappearing Wetlands*. Chicago: Children's Press, 1992.

Morgan, Ann Haven. *Field Book of Ponds and Streams*. New York: Putnam, 1930.

Rood, Ronald. *Beachcombers All*. Shelburne, VT: New England Press, 1990.

Sabin, Francine. *Swamps and Marshes*. Mahwah, NJ: Troll Associates, 1985.

Stone, Lynn M. *Marshes and Swamps*. Chicago: Children's Press, 1983.